Walks around the Lorton Valley

(from the Wheatsheaf Inn)

by

David Ramshaw

Useful Information

ACCESS AND COUNTRY CODE -
The description of a route in this book does not necessarily imply a right of way. Please respect the country code. **DO NOT** climb over or damage walls, fences or hedges. **DO NOT** deposit litter, take it home with you. Take care not to frighten livestock. **DO** follow marked paths wherever possible, using stiles and gates. **DO** close gates after you and **DO** keep your dog under close control, **ON A LEAD** (if he is not fully trained to stay by you and completely ignore sheep).

On the Hills: it is essential that anyone intending to venture onto the hills is properly equipped for the conditions that they may encounter. The following items of equipment are, in my opinion, the minimum necessary for a fine weather trip onto the Lakeland Fells:

Strong walking boots, walking trousers or breeches (not cotton jeans), windproof anorak with hood, spare sweater, gloves, extra emergency food, first aid kit, map, compass, torch, whistle, a survival bag and of course a rucksack to put them all in. Nowadays a mobile phone etc. is useful in case of accident, but you should not rely on that alone for navigation.

More information: a free leaflet is available, from the Information and Visitor Centres throughout the National Park, entitled 'Safety on the Fells.'

The proximity of the lakeland mountains to the Irish Sea and the prevailing westerly winds can lead to sudden and dramatic changes in the weather. It is all too common to set out for the tops in warm and pleasant conditions to be confronted, sometime later, with driving rain and a cold blustery wind. Do **NOT** get caught out. Go properly equipped.

Weatherline: bringing you the Lake District Weather Forecast
Link: http://www.lakedistrictweatherline.co.uk/ or just type Lake District Weather into your search engine.

OS map Explorer OL4 -North Western Area - English Lakes - 1:2500 scale is recommended for the walks in this book.

The Wheatsheaf Inn, Low Lorton

This book came about as a result of a conversation between myself and Mark and Jackie of the Wheatsheaf Inn, Low Lorton. Mark mentioned that visitors staying at his camping and caravan park often asked if he had information on local walks from the village and that it would be useful to have a small guidebook describing local walks in the area, starting from his premises.

I have written general guides in the past for the higher Lakeland fells including the local history, so it was decided to produce a small guide that described the routes around the valley through pictures rather than just written notes. Children can have fun finding the next waypoint from the pictures. Where possible, information on the history of the area is included

Whilst researching the book between 2011 and 2017 my friends Ken and Pete, often walked routes with me (and the dogs) and, apart from being welcome walking companions, they provided human interest in the photographs of gates, stiles etc.. Thank you Ken and Pete.

Although living in Carlisle, relatively close to Lorton, we occasionally camped at the Wheatsheaf site. Thank you Mark for the free camping.

Walks in this guide

Most of the walks described follow public footpaths around the valley and do not include much, if any, climbing. For these walks walking boots are preferable if you wish to keep your feet dry. However, I have also included a few walks which take one up onto the surrounding fells where walking boots, windproof clothing and navigation aids as described on the previous page could well be essential.

The Green at Boonbeck

Several of the walks from the village start and finish at the village green adjacent to Boonbeck so I will start by describing how to get there from the Wheatsheaf Inn.

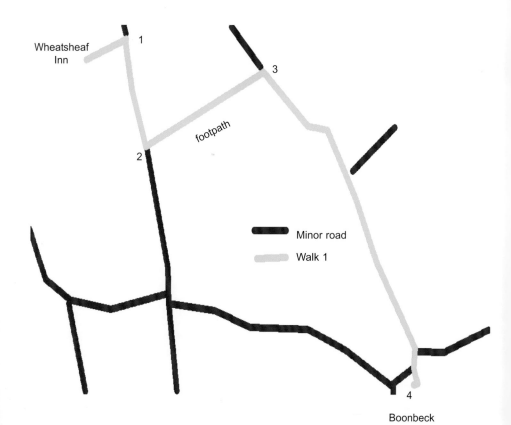

Walk 1: From the Wheatsheaf Inn to Boonbeck

20 Minutes: level walk - minor road and footpath.

Leave the Wheatsheaf camping site via the gate at the eastern end of the camping field (1) and turn right onto the road (care).

Follow the road south, past the church, to arrive in about 120m at a kissing gate on the left hand side (2).

Pass through the gate and follow the footpath in an easterly direction for about 250m to reach another kissing gate at the next minor road (3).

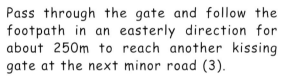

Turn right and follow the road for a further 600m. Along the route note the fine row of cottages which, according to resident Sally, was originally one house, a byre and a barn built in the late 1600's. Then in the 1800's they were bought by Lorton Park (the 18th Century house opposite as estate cottages and Gothicised

At the road junction turn left to pass over the Boonbeck by the road bridge. On the right is the village green with seat next to the Boonbeck. This is the starting point for several of the walks in this book.

There is some interesting local history here. The large building backing onto the beck is the original Jennings Brewery and to the left of that building is the Lorton Yew, immortalised by Wordsworth in his poem "The Pride of Lorton Vale".

The Lorton yew and Jennings old brewery
(from the seat on the green)

Walk 2: Boonbeck to The Hope via High Swinside, return by Low Swinside.

2 Hours - A moderate walk with some climbing (120m) to the highest point at High Swinside. The route includes minor roads, farm tracks and public footpaths across farmland. Total distance - 4.5 Km.

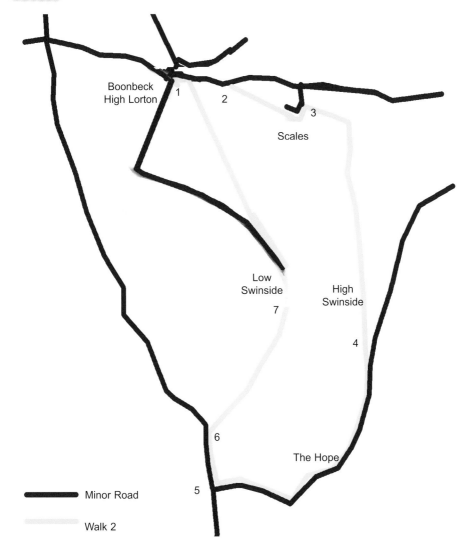

From the seat on the Green take the minor road to the east signposted Boonbeck and Scales. In 200m look for a public footpath sign on the right indicating an iron kissing gate in the hedge (2).

Pass through the gate and follow the footpath to the left of the fence to arrive at Scales in about 300m.

Pass through the iron gate to join the road and follow it for about 50m past the farm and to the left where a public footpath sign will be seen on the right hand side (3).

Follow this path which (after 150m) improves to a lovely grassy lane as it bears right towards High Swinside Farm. Total length about 900m.

Join the metalled road which leads round the left of the farm and on up

to a junction with a minor road (4). The road junction is the highest point on this route and fine views are to be had ahead, towards the Buttermere Fells.

Turn right at Hopebeck junction onto the minor road signposted to Cockermouth (71 cycle route).

Follow this path across the field through the gap between the stone wall and a wire fence and walk on across

Bear right at the junction and continue south, downhill, past 'The Hope' farm to the road junction at Hopebeck 1 km ahead (5).

Follow this road for 250m to reach a left hand bend in the road. Here a public footpath on the right is accessed through a field gate (6).

the next field looking for a stile in the wire fence.
Continue on towards the trees at the

next field boundary. Here there is a plank bridge across a stream with a stile set into the wall beyond.

Keeping the large oak on your right continue straight across the next field towards Low Swinside to pass through a gate followed by a stone

wall on your left to reach a leafy track leading to the farm. The walk from the road (6) to Low Swinside (7) is about 650m.

Follow the track which leads downhill in front of the farmhouse towards High Mill for 250m and look out for a stile in the wall on the right with

7

stone steps leading up to it.
Climb this stile into the field beyond. Looking to the north there is a large stone barn at the end of the field. Walk across the field to the corner post seen well to the right of the barn. This leads directly to a stile into the next field. The person in the

photo is looking directly towards this stile. Climb the stile and cross the bridge over the stream beyond to continue the walk. If the path is indistinct just keep the field boundary on your right. Soon you should see the buildings of High Lorton through

the trees in the distance.
Walk towards these buildings and, as you approach the next field boundary, you may find the grasses quite high. If you push through it you will find

the next stile with a plastic tube protecting walkers from the barbed wire. Climb this stile which takes you through to the last field before High Lorton.

Walk on towards the white house in the distance, crossing a stream halfway across the field. Keep the wooden fence on your right and look for the footpath sign and stile in the stone wall which takes you back to your startpoint.

Walk 3: Boonbeck via Highmill bridge to High Whitbeck bridge, then along a minor road to return via High Mill (short walk) or return by Low Swinside and High Mill (longer walk).

Short walk - 45min - 2km
Longer walk - 1H 15min - 3.5 km

along footpaths, farm tracks and a minor road. A level route.

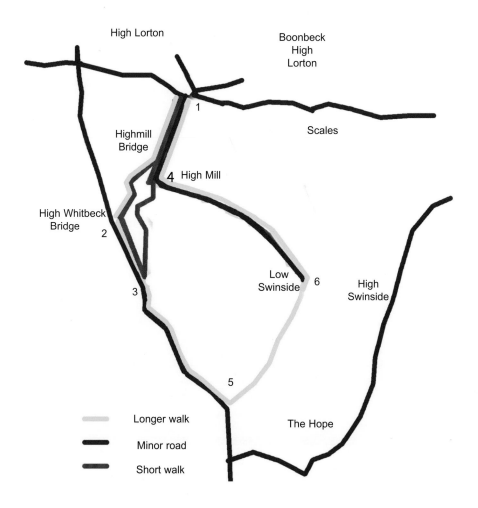

From the seat on the Green walk back over the bridge to the road junction and turn left. Walk to the end of the old 'Jennings Brewery' building on your left and turn left into the road marked cul-de-sac, passing the house 'Yew Tree View' on your left.

Continue down the road for about 250m to reach Highmill bridge.

Just before the bridge look for a footpath sign on your right. Climb over the stone stile in the wall and

follow this pleasant path with the stream on the left and Highmill on the other bank.

After crossing two more stiles (one with a 'dog slot' in it) the path emerges onto the road at High Whitbeck bridge via another stile (2).

Turn left along this minor road and in a further 125m there is a footpath to the left signposted High Mill. If you are doing the short walk turn left here and continue along this shaded lane to High Mill (4 on the Walk 3 map). From there return along the road to the start point at Boon Beck.l

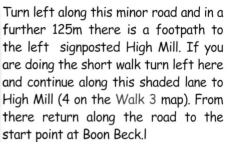

For the longer walk carry straight on for a further 900m when you will reach a stile on the left which featured in Walk 2. (see picture below). The route from there to Low Swinside is repeated here . Follow this path across the field through the gap between the stone

wall and a wire fence and walk on across the next field looking for a stile in the wire fence. Continue on towards the trees at the next field boundary. Here there is a plank bridge across a

stream with a stile set into the wall beyond. Keeping the large oak on your right continue straight across the next field towards Low Swinside to pass through a gate followed by a stone wall on your left to reach a

leafy track leading to the farm. The walk from the road (5) to Low Swinside (6) is about 650m.

From Low Swinside follow the minor road back to High Mill and thence to the green at Boon Beck (about 1.5km).

Walk 4: Low Lorton to Low Fell via Thackthwaite return by the same route (shorter walk). or return via Fellbarrow (longer walk).

Good walking boots required.

Shorter walk - total distance - about 10km. Time 3 hours.
1.7km along minor roads to Thackthwaite.
300m of ascent in 3.2km of climbing to Low Fell summit.
Longer walk - total distance - about 13km
As above to the summit of Low Fell with an extra 100m of climbing to Fellbarrow. Time 3.5 to 4 hours.

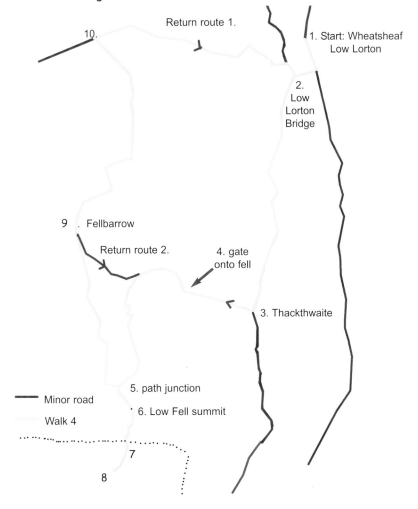

Return route 1.

10.

1. Start: Wheatsheaf
   Low Lorton

2.
Low
Lorton
Bridge

9 . Fellbarrow

Return route 2.

4. gate
onto fell

3. Thackthwaite

5. path junction

—— Minor road

6. Low Fell summit

Walk 4

7

8

Leave the campsite by the entrance beside the Wheatsheaf (1) and turn left onto the road through the village to arrive in 200m at a crossroads. Turn right towards Thackthwaite and cross the new bridge over the River Cocker which replaced the original stone bridge built in 1843 and destroyed in the 2009 floods (2).

Turn left at the junction and follow the road for 2km to the hamlet of Thackwaite. Walk on through the village to Thackwaite Farm on the right (3).

Turn right here. Go through the double gates on the concrete road and follow the footpath up onto the fell.

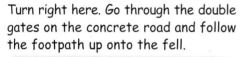

The path follows a beck for the first 100m and then rises gently for a further 400m, passing along the edge of two fields to reach a field gate with kissing gate, leading onto the open fell, under Watching Crag (4).

Ignore the main track to the left and follow the path to the right which rises steadily to the north as it curves left round the end of the Watching Crag, eventually travelling south.
After 750m of gentle climbing the path approaches the head of a small

valley It then turns left to zig zag up the fell, as the ascent steepens (see the photograph below taken from the opposite side of the valley).

In a further 500m a gate in a wire fence on the ridge is reached (5). A faint path leads off to the right here towards Fellbarrow. Ignore this and continue through the gate and on towards the stone cairn (6) marking the summit of Low Fell with a

lovely view to the south over Crummock Water. This may be the highest point on the ridge but there is another viewpoint if time allows.

The path continues on past the summit cairn to descend to a stile with a dog flap (7). The path then

rises to a second summit. From there the second viewpoint, the Bield, can be seen 250m ahead.
Below: The route to the Bield (8)

A dam for Loweswater lead mine was built in the high valley to the west of this ridge. The dam burst in heavy rain in July 1828 causing the death of two people at a farm near Loweswater. The remains of the dam can be seen if you walk to the west (away from the path) to see into the valley.

You now have two options:
Return by the same route (shorter walk).
Return via Fellbarrow (longer walk).

For the longer walk return to the gate at the path junction (5).
Pass through the gate and turn left along the path which curves round to the right to eventually meet a drystone wall and fence which follows

the ridge, climbing with undulations, to the summit of Fellbarrow in a distance of about 1.5km.

Although relatively low at 416m Fellbarrow is a wonderful viewpoint for the Solway Estuary, the Dumfriesshire hills to the north and the lakeland hills of Whiteside and Grasmoor to the south-east.

Below: panorama from Fellbarrow **Northern** - above **Southern** - below.

Return from Fellbarrow summit

There is no clearly marked path on the OS map for the return to Low Lorton bridge. There are two routes to consider.

1. A slightly longer route, making the total walk circular, leads to the north and, once off the open fell, follows tracks and very minor roads back to Low Lorton (about 5 km).

2. A steeper route, of 2.5 km down to Thackthwaite can be taken with a further 2 km along the road to Low Lorton; 3 km of which involves retracing your steps.

Route 2.

From the summit cairn cross over the fence and retrace your steps south down the hill (the fence on your right) to the bottom of the dip between Fellbarrow and Smithy Fell. Here a faint path leads steeply to the left.

Follow this path which becomes less steep down the slope towards the end of Watching Crag in the distance. After a series of ups and downs the wide path under Watching Crag used

on the ascent is reached. Turn left and retrace your steps down to

Thackthwaite Farm.

6

To return to Low Lorton follow the road north for a further 2km.

Route 1. (circular route).
From the summit cairn follow the path as it descends to the north for about 70m to a fence . Cross the stile and continue a further 330m as it descends to a ladder stile (10). Climb the stile and turn immediately right towards another stile 40m ahead.

Cross this stile and turn left to follow the fence over the brow of the hill. Descend the hill with the fence/collapsed wall on your left for a further 360 m to reach a farm track, shown below.

Turn left along this track, passing through the gate, as the stile is broken). Please close the gate behind you.

The track now leads northwards passing through a large field as shown on the right, descending and rising again to follow the field wall, to a locked gate.

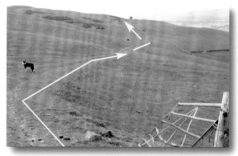

Stone steps are set into the wall, and even large collie dogs can slip underneath the gate.

The track is now bounded on both sides with fences and walls and gradually descends to a minor road linking Low Lorton to

Mosser. Turn right onto this road which follows an undulating

course as it gradually descends back towards Low Lorton.

A junction is reached at Low Lorton.
Turn right here to see   Low

Lorton bridge directly in front of you.
Cross the bridge and turn left to return to the Wheatsheaf.

There is no easy route to the summit of Kirkfell without some road walking. The route below uses sections of public footpath, roads and (from High Side) two fields to reach the open fell.

Up to waymark 3 on the map below is identical to Walk 1 in this book. so the walk description will start from that point.

Walk 5: Low Lorton to Kirk Fell via High Side return by the same route (shorter walk).
or return via Graystones (longer walk).

Good walking boots required.
Shorter walk - total distance - about 5km. Time 2.5 hours.
1km along paths and minor roads to High Side
360m of ascent in 1.5 km of climbing to Kirk Fell summit.

Longer walk - total distance - about 6.5km
As above to the summit of Kirk Fell with an extra 16m of climbing in 500m to Graystones. Time 3.5 hours.

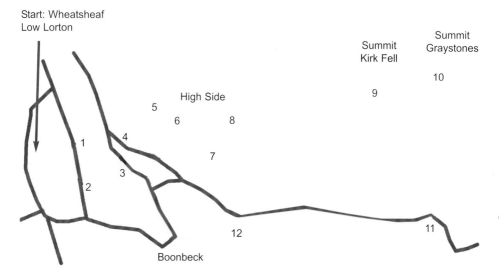

Start: Wheatsheaf
Low Lorton

Summit
Kirk Fell

Summit
Graystones

High Side

Boonbeck

The route from the Wheatsheaf follows Route 1 as far as the Kissing gate (3) on the map.

Cross the road, pass through the gate opposite and follow the path across the field to the opposite corner to emerge ot another road.

Cross this road to follow the farm road (4) towards High Side.

Ignore the turn off to Terrace Farm and keep right past Fernwood.

Continue straight on to reach some dilapidated farm buildings (5) and, a little further on, the old house at High Side.

The track curves round the house to meet a farm gate (6).

Pass through the gate and carry on straight ahead across the field to an open gate with a lone tree to the right.

Walk on across the next field to the gate in a stone wall leading onto the open fell, shown by the arrow on picture (7).
Pass through the gate onto the open fell and follow the track climbing to the left.
(Please close this gate behind you if it is closed when you arrive).

In a short distance the track splits just before the fenced of plantation. Take the track to the right leading uphill (8).

Note: The original route to Kirkfell turned sharp left at the gate (6), and followed the stone wall for 200m to pass through an old iron gate onto the fell. This is not now possible as that part of the fell has been enclosed and planted with trees to reduce erosion.

Follow the track up the hill, eventually passing through a gap in a collapsed wall .

The track gradually becomes less distinct as shown on the left.

Continue upwards towards the highest point on the skyline, keeping on the ridge with the ravine of Wythe Gill to the left, as shown.

Only two large stones mark the summit of Kirk Fell (438m) (9) which is reached after 1.3 km of climbing from High Side.

However the summit provides fine views

Looking west one can see Low Lorton and the Wheatsheaf Inn.

The view to the north east towards Wythop Moss and Bassenthwaite.

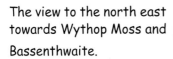

Return either by the same route - or Via Graystones

Return via Graystones:

Continue eastwards from the summit of Kirk Fell to drop down into a dip before rising again to the summit of Greystones with a stone wall falling away to the south as shown below.
At the summit of Greystones (10) again there is just a small pile of stones.

From the summit a drystone wall leads south down towards Scawgill bridge.

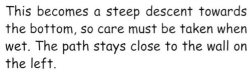

This becomes a steep descent towards the bottom, so care must be taken when wet. The path stays close to the wall on the left.

As the road is approached the path leaves the wall and passes beneath an old quarry to reach the path from the Scawgill Bridge to Spout Force waterfall. From here (11) the road must be walked back to High Lorton. Take care and walk to face oncoming traffic along the B5292.

In 1.1 km the junction (12) is reached. Continue straight on down the steep narrow side road on the left to arrive back in High Lorton near Boon Beck. Turn right and return to the Wheatsheaf as shown on Walk 1 (page 5).

Walk 6: Low Lorton to Kirk Fell - longer route - via High Armaside and around Harrot Fell.
Return routes as per walk 5 (page 27).

Good walking boots required.
Lorton to Kirkfell summit - distance 6km - including 360m of ascent in 4 km of climbing to Kirk Fell summit.

Time to summit   about 2.5 hours.

Return times -   via Graystones - about 1 hour 15 min.
                 via High Side - about 50 minutes.

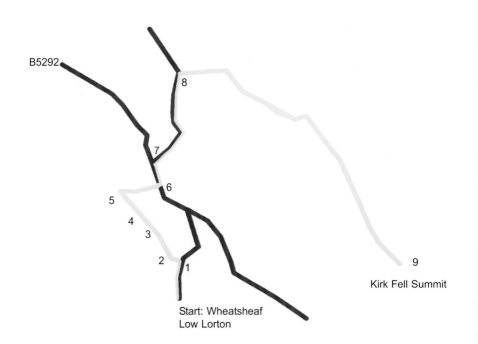

Walk northwards from the Wheatsheaf about 100m to the Low Lorton sign at the entrance to the village. Here, adjacent to the field gate on the left, is a stile giving access into the field. Follow the edge of the field to a gate (2) leading into a much larger field.

Turn northwards again and follow the edge of the field for about 250 m to a gate at the top right (3)

Continue on into the next field walking towards the central line of trees with a footpath gate set into a wire fence. (4).

Pass through the gate and follow the fence to a gate set into the drystone wall ahead (5).

Pass through the gate in the wall to immediately encounter another gate in the wire fence on your right. See below.

Pass through this second gate and follow the field edge on your right to meet the B5292 road at (6), where there is a gate and footpath sign to Stanger.

Take care on accessing the road. Turn left and, facing oncoming traffic, walk about 250 to a minor road junction on the right (7).

Take this quiet side road to the right and in 400m the road turns left past High Armaside. It then climbs steadily to reach, in a further 300m or so, sheet metal farm entrance gates on the right (8).

Do not be deterred. A public footpath sign points the way. If the gates are closed then lift the bar to open them and close them behind you as animals are sometimes in the yard.

If the gate at the other end of the yard is closed there is a small gate to the left (9).

Continue on up the track which eventually swings right as it climbs round the back of Harrot, passing through two more gates before the open fell is reached (10),

This is about 1.4km from the road.

open fell

Once on the open fell a faint path leads south towards the rounded summit of Kirk Fell. On the way a fence is encountered adjacent to a collapsed drystone wall. (11). Look for the stile to cross the fence and continue on and upwards to arrive at the summit marked by two stones (12)

Return routes as per walk 5 (page 27).

About the author

David Ramshaw is an author and local publisher. He began writing Lakeland guides with local history in the 1990s and has since won several 'Lakeland Book of the Year' awards for books he has published. David has walked the Lake District for more than sixty years and has a wealth of interesting tales to tell. He is a committee member of the Outdoor Writers and Photographers Guild. David has an honours degree in physics and chemistry and taught physics for more than thirty years. He lives in Carlisle.